OUTLINES ON THE HOLY SPIRIT

Croft M. Pentz

BAKER BOOK HOUSE
Grand Rapids, Michigan

Fifth printing, March 1985

Copyright 1978
by Baker Book House Company
ISBN: 0-8010-7029-5

Printed in the United States of America

CONTENTS

CONTENTS

PREFACE

God is not the author of confusion and does not want His people ignorant concerning the Spirit. Therefore God's Word concerning this member of the Godhead must be taught. Being a Pentecostal minister, I see the extremes in thought and practice among Pentecostal churches and charismatic groups, as well as in non-Pentecostal churches. Many of these differences are caused by a lack of teaching and understanding, others by rejection of the truth.

Extreme viewpoints among those *receiving* the charismatic experience are: (1) Mysticism. There is nothing mystic about the Holy Spirit. (2) Spiritual pride. Some feel that because they have certain spiritual gifts they are better than others. (3) Feeling of perfection. Perfection will come only when we are with the Lord in heaven. (4) Emotion without God's Word. Emotional experiences are of little value unless we live according to God's Word.

Extreme viewpoints among those *rejecting* the charismatic experiences are: (1) A closed mind. Many are unwilling to break tradition. (2) Wild charges. Many accuse those who speak in tongues of being immature, insane, or demon possessed. (3) Danger of blasphemy. No person knows all concerning the work and moving of the Holy Spirit.

Paul commanded all Christians to be filled with the Spirit (Eph. 5:18). Jesus told His followers to tarry in Jerusalem until they had this power (Luke 24:49). All God's people need to know what it means to be filled with the Spirit, to have the fruits of the Spirit in daily operation, and to use the gifts of the Spirit.

I have enjoyed preparing and delivering these basic outlines on the Holy Spirit. They have been a blessing to myself and to my congregation. May these outlines be helpful to Christian workers in enlightening others on the personality and work of the Holy Spirit.

—Croft M. Pentz

1.

THE SEVEN SPIRITS OF GOD

Though the Holy Spirit has been given many names, such as Spirit of God, Spirit of Christ, and Holy Ghost, He is one. (Note the words of John in Revelation 1:4; 4:5; 5:6.) The number *seven* in the Bible is always considered a perfect number.

I. **THE SPIRIT OF GRACE**
   Grace is the unmerited favor of God. In other words, it is receiving something we do not deserve. (Note Hebrews 10:19).
   A. Saved by grace—Ephesians 2:8, 9.
   B. Sustained by grace—II Timothy 2:1

II. **THE SPIRIT OF LIFE**
   A. Creation—Genesis 1:2. The Spirit always produces life. He produces both physical as well as spiritual life.
   B. Conversion—II Corinthians 5:17. This new life is nothing that we do on our own; it is what God has already done.
   C. Confidence—Romans 8:2. The Spirit sets us free from the law and gives us new life in Christ.

III. **THE SPIRIT OF ADOPTION**
   All are born in sin—Romans 3:23. Salvation makes us children of God. We are adopted into His family.
   A. Spirit of adoption—Romans 8:15
   B. Sincere approach—Hebrews 4:16
   C. Spiritual acceptance—Galatians 4:7

IV. **THE SPIRIT OF HOLINESS**
   Holiness is not a drudgery. It is a positive way of conducting our lives. Holiness is something we practice.
   A. Spirit of burning—Isaiah 4:4. The Spirit burns up all sin and produces holiness.

B. Spirit of holiness—Romans 1:4. Jesus, the holy Son of God, set an example for us to be holy.

V. THE SPIRIT OF SUPPLICATION—Romans 8:26-27
A. Spirit—v. 26a. He knows and helps our infirmities.
B. Supernatural—v. 26b. The Spirit prays through us.
C. Searching—v. 27a. He is divine, knowing God's will.
D. Saints—v. 27b. The Spirit prays for the Christian according to God's will.

VI. THE SPIRIT OF TRUTH
A. Person of truth—John 14:6. Christ is the truth.
B. Personality of the truth—John 15:26. The Comforter, the Truth.
C. Power of the truth—John 8:26, 32. Sets men free.

We must have truth. (See Hosea 4:6). The lack of knowledge or understanding may be caused by rejection of truth.

VII. THE SPIRIT OF GLORY
A. The reproach—I Peter 4:14. Being reproached for the name of Christ is proof that the spirit of glory is upon us. When we are reproached for Christ the Spirit is glorified. Thus we should be happy.
B. The reckoning—Romans 8:18. Our sufferings are not worthy to be compared with the glory of God.

Stephen was glorified when he was stoned to death (Acts 7:55). Christ received him into heaven.

As a human body has various parts with different names and functions, so the Spirit has various names, yet is one Spirit, doing the work of God.

2.

THE HOLY SPIRIT AND THE TRINITY

I. THE HOLY SPIRIT IS GOD

Note these characteristics:

A. Eternal—Hebrews 9:14. He has always existed.

B. Omnipresent—Psalm 139:7-12. He is everywhere.

C. Omniscient—I Corinthians 2:10. He knows everything.

D. Omnipotent—Acts 10:38. He is all powerful.

E. Holy—I Corinthians 6:11; I Peter 1:2. The holiness of the Spirit purifies Christians.

F. True—John 14:17. The Holy Spirit is truth as Christ is the truth. (See I John 5:6.)

G. Self existent, yet one with God and Christ—Romans 8:2. (Note also II Corinthians 3:3, the Spirit of the living God.)

H. Glorious—I Peter 4:14. He is the "spirit of glory and of God."

II. THE HOLY SPIRIT AND GOD

A. Spirit of God—Genesis 1:1, 2; I Corinthians 3:16

B. Spirit of the Lord—Judges 3:10; Isaiah 11:2

C. His Spirit—Isaiah 48:16

D. My Spirit—Genesis 6:3

E. Thy Spirit—Psalm 139:7

F. Thy good Spirit—Nehemiah 9:20

G. The holy spirit—Psalm 51:11

H. Spirit of the Lord God—Isaiah 61:1

I. Spirit of your Father—Matthew 10:20

J. Spirit of the Lord—Luke 4:18

K. Spirit of him—Romans 8:11

L. Spirit of our God—I Corinthians 6:11

M. Spirit of the living God—II Corinthians 3:3

N. Holy Spirit of God—Ephesians 4:30

III. THE HOLY SPIRIT AND GOD'S SON

A. The Spirit of Christ—Romans 8:9

1. Dwelling in the Spirit. "But ye are not in the flesh, but in the Spirit, if so be that the Spirit of God dwell in you." As we are in Christ, Christ is in us. (Note Paul's words in II Corinthians 5:17.)
2. Divine Spirit. "Now if any man have not the Spirit of Christ, he is none of his."
B. The Spirit of His Son—Galatians 4:6
1. The Spirit. "And because ye are sons, God hath sent forth the Spirit of his Son into your hearts."
2. The Son. "Crying, Abba, Father." When born into the family of God, we become His sons (John 1:12).

3.

THE SPIRIT IN GENESIS

"And God said, Let us [God, Christ, Holy Spirit] make man in our image" (Gen. 1:26). The Trinity is eternal. The Holy Spirit was present at and assisted in the creation. The Holy Spirit plays a very important part in the Book of Genesis. Listed are just a few areas in which He has a part.

I. **THE SPIRIT IN CREATION**
"When God began creating the heavens and the earth, the earth was at first a shapeless, chaotic mass, with the Spirit of God brooding over the dark vapors" (Gen. 1:1, 2, LB).
A. Creating power—John 1:3. All things were made by God. The earth and universe did not just happen; they were created by God. All things, including man, did not evolve; they were created by God.
B. Controlling power—Colossians 1:16. All things in heaven and earth were created by Him. "He was before all else began and it is His power

that holds everything together" (Col. 1:17, LB).

C. Continuing power—Psalm 104:30. "Then you send your Spirit, and new life is born to replenish all the living of the earth" (LB).

II. THE SPIRIT AND CARELESSNESS

God gave men 120 years to hear and believe Noah's preaching. However, after 120 years, God's patience ran out and the flood came (Gen. 6–8).

A. Resisting the Spirit's pleading. As Noah built the ark, he warned men of the coming judgment by preaching to them.

B. Resisting the Spirit's plan. Noah told men to come into the ark. Men refused, but the animals obeyed. It has been said that an estimated 137 million people lived on the earth at this time, and only eight escaped.

C. Resisting the Spirit's preaching. The people heard Noah's preaching, but resisted it. (See Proverbs 29:1.)

D. Resisting the Spirit's protection. The ark was the only way of escape (Christ is our ark, John 14:6).

III. THE SPIRIT AND CONTROL

A. Rejection—Genesis 39:7-14. Joseph refused to commit adultery with Potiphar's wife. Though the Ten Commandments were not yet given, Joseph knew this was sin. The Spirit showed Joseph this was wrong.

B. Responsibility. Because Joseph refused to sin, Potiphar's wife told a lie about Joseph and he was put into prison. But God was with Joseph and had a job for him to do.

1. Selection—Genesis 41:38-39. Joseph became the second top man in the land. It took him sixteen years to do this, but he was patient.

2. Spirit—Genesis 41:38. The Spirit of God was in him.

4.

THE PROMISED HOLY SPIRIT
Joel 2:28, 29

Many promises are given about the Holy Spirit in both the Old and New testaments. Some of these promises apply to us today. The Holy Spirit was sent by God to help men be better and stronger Christians. After Jesus ascended into heaven, He sent the Comforter who abides with God's people.

I. **THE PROMISES IN PROPHECY**
   A. Major prophet—Isaiah 28:11. This prophecy was given 712 years before Christ was born. The prophet here is speaking about the forthcoming day of Pentecost (Acts 2:1-4). Stammering lips precedes speaking in tongues.
   B. Minor prophet—Joel 2:28, 29. This prophecy was given 800 years before Christ's birth. This promise would come true on the day of Pentecost. Peter confirms this in his sermon, after the Holy Spirit had descended (Acts 2:17, 18).

II. **THE PROMISES OF POWER**
   A. Power to wait—Luke 24:49. Seeking God almost always involves waiting. The prophet Jeremiah tells how we will find God if we search for Him with all our hearts (Jer. 29:13). Power is always available to those who take time to wait before God.
   B. Promise to witness—Acts 1:8. The witness would be fourfold:
      1. Jerusalem—home town
      2. Judea—home state
      3. Samaria—home country
      4. Uttermost part of the earth—foreign missions

The Bible speaks of the four corners of the world (Isaiah 11:12). This could mean taking the gospel to the north, south, east, and west.

III. THE PROMISE IN PREACHING—Mark 16:17-18

A. Promise—vv. 17-18. What this promised power would do:
1. Cast out devils. Satan's oppression, depression, and possession.
2. Speak with new tongues—Acts 2:1-4.
3. Take up serpents (by mistake) and not be hurt.
4. Drink any poisonous liquids (by accident) and not be hurt.
5. Lay hands upon the sick, and the sick will recover.

B. Proof—vv. 19-20
1. Ascension—v. 19. Christ ascends into heaven (cf. Acts 1:11).
2. Power—v. 20. Christ's followers go forward with power, performing the things He promised in vv. 17-18.

IV. THE PROMISE AFTER PENTECOST—Acts 2:39

A. The past. The gift of the Holy Spirit was given to those who asked.

B. The present. The gift of the Holy Spirit is given today, to all who ask for it and who meet the requirements of God's Word for receiving it.

Some try to explain away the Holy Spirit and speaking in tongues. Some say that it is not for today, and use Scriptures out of context to back their teaching. However, even cults can use Scriptures in this way to prove their teachings.

V. CLAIMING THE PROMISE

If a person claims the promises of God, he will receive the gift of the Holy Spirit. The Holy Spirit was given so men could know and serve God in a better way. God wants men to know how to:

A. Walk in the Spirit—Galatians 5:16

B. Witness in the Spirit—Acts 1:8

C. Worship in the Spirit—John 4:24

5.

SYMBOLS OF THE HOLY SPIRIT

There are many symbols for the Holy Spirit, however, keep in mind that the Holy Spirit is a person and a member of the Trinity (Matt. 28:19). Always refer to the Spirit as He.

I. **DOVE SYMBOL**—gentleness
    A. Pleasure—Matt. 3:16-17. God is pleased as the Holy Spirit descends upon Christ in the form of a dove.
    B. Patience—Matt. 10:16. The Holy Spirit is never harmful; He always helps.

II. **SEAL SYMBOL**—ownership
    A. Past—John 6:37. We have been sealed by God.
    B. Proof. "And because of what Christ did, all you others too, who heard the Good News about how to be saved, and trusted Christ, were marked as belonging to Christ by the Holy Spirit, who long ago had been promised to all of us Christians. His presence within us is God's guarantee that he really will give us all that he promised; and the Spirit's seal upon us means that God has already purchased us and that he guarantees to bring us to himself..." (Eph. 1:13, 14, LB).

III. **OIL SYMBOL**—approval
    A. Anointed for preaching—Luke 4:18. The Spirit anointed Christ for preaching as a sign of God's approval.
    B. Anointed with power—Acts 10:38. Christ showed His power through action.

IV. **FIRE SYMBOL**—purification
    A. Power—Matthew 3:11. Power to baptize in the Holy Spirit. This is a different experience than salvation and water baptism.
    B. Proof—Acts 2:3. Cloven tongues of fire rested upon all that were present.

V. **RAIN SYMBOL**—refreshing
   A. Refreshing—Psalm 72:6. Rain always refreshes the thirsty.
   B. Results—Hosea 6:3. Latter rain is always good for crops.

VI. **WIND SYMBOL**—being invisible
   A. Supernatural power—John 3:8. Those born of the Spirit receive the supernatural power of the Holy Spirit.
   B. Strength—Acts 2:2. The Holy Spirit came with the sound of a rushing mighty wind on the day of Pentecost.

VI. **RIVER SYMBOL**—abundance
   A. Plenty—John 7:38. Rivers of living water will flow out of men as they believe in Christ.
   B. Prosperity—Psalm 1:3. Righteous men are like trees planted by the water.

VIII. **DEW SYMBOL**—fertility
   A. Request—Genesis 27:28. The Spirit always gives men God's best.
   B. Refreshment—Isaiah 18:4. Spiritual dew refreshes spiritually thirsty souls.

IX. **WATER SYMBOL**—effectiveness
   A. Cleansing—John 3:5. The Spirit brings the new birth.
   B. Comparison—John 4:14. Jesus is the water of life.

6.

THE HOLY SPIRIT
IN THE LIFE OF CHRIST
Matthew 4:16

Christ is a member of the Trinity. He is the divine Son of God, as well as the human Son of Man. He was dependent on the Holy Spirit while He was on the earth. By this, He set a good example for all to follow.

I. **AT CHRIST'S BIRTH**
  A. Favor—Matthew 1:20. Mary was favored by the Holy Spirit to become the mother of the Son of God.
  B. Fulfillment—Isaiah 7:14. Isaiah's prophecy given 700 years before Christ's birth was now being fulfilled.

II. **AT CHRIST'S BAPTISM**
  A. Symbol—Matthew 3:16. The Holy Spirit descended upon Christ in the form of a dove.
  B. Son—Matthew 3:17. God voiced approval of His Son because Christ obeyed His Father.

Jesus did not really need water baptism, but He was willing to set an example for all to follow.

III. **IN CHRIST'S MINISTRY**
  A. The preparation—Mark 1:12. Christ was led by the Spirit into the wilderness to be tempted. The Spirit did not tempt Christ, but led Him to be tempted. This was a test for Christ.
  B. The power—Luke 4:14. After forty days of being tempted, he returned in the power of the Spirit. Christ had overcome the test as the Spirit helped Him resist the many temptations.
  C. The preaching—Luke 4:18. Christ preached in the power of the Holy Spirit. This is a fulfillment of Isaiah 61:1-2.

IV. **AT CHRIST'S CRUCIFIXION**
Christ offered Himself to God, perfect and without any sin (Heb. 9:14).
  A. The Spirit helped Christ to submit (Phil. 2:8). Humbling Himself, Christ became obedient to the death of the cross.
  B. Christ suffered as man (Mark 14:36). He was willing to do God's will, even if it meant suffering upon the cross.

V. **IN CHRIST'S RESURRECTION**
  A. Spiritual power—Romans 1:4.

B. Spiritual perfection—Romans 8:11. His Spirit will quicken also our spirits.
C. Spiritual pardon. "The Scriptures tell us that the first man, Adam, was given a natural, human body, but Christ is more than that, for he was life-giving Spirit" (I Cor. 15:45, LB).

VI. IN CHRIST'S ASCENSION
A. Power of Christ's ascension—John 14:1-3, Acts 1:11. The Holy Spirit transported Him to heaven.
B. Promise of our ascension—I Thessalonians 4:13-18 (cf. Acts 1:11).

As Christ depended upon the Holy Spirit, so we need to do. As the Spirit anointed Christ to speak, so He will anoint us to witness. As the Spirit empowered Christ to overcome temptation, so will He help us to overcome.

7.

THE BAPTISM OF THE HOLY SPIRIT
Acts 2:1-4

When one accepts Christ as Savior, the Holy Spirit dwells within him. However, one does not have the fulness of the Spirit until he experiences the baptism of the Holy Spirit. When one speaks in tongues, it is an overflow of the Spirit. The baptism of the Holy Spirit is different than salvation and water baptism. Spirit baptism was a normal happening in the early church.

I. THE PURPOSE OF THE BAPTISM
A. Power—Luke 24:49. The disciples were commissioned to carry on the work of Christ. They needed the Spirit's power to accomplish this work.
B. Preaching—Acts 1:8. When filled with the Holy Spirit, one is empowered to do God's work.

The power of the baptism of the Holy Spirit is not to be gained for selfish reasons, but is to be used for the glory of God.

II. THE PROMISE OF THE BAPTISM

A. Prophecy—Joel 2:28-29. This promise was fulfilled on the day of Pentecost (cf. Acts 2:1-4). This promise has been fulfilled throughout the years, even up to the present time.

B. Promise—Acts 2:4. These 120 people prayed for ten days in the upper room, claiming the promise of Joel 2:28-29.

C. People—Acts 2:39. Note that the promise is to *all* people. It did not end with the disciples or early church leaders. There are no Scriptures to prove that the baptism of the Holy Spirit ended with the disciples.

III. THE PARTICULARS OF THE BAPTISM

A. Christians—Acts 8:16. These people were already born again, but had not received the Holy Spirit. Jesus told Christians to wait for this experience (Luke 24:49; Acts 1:4).

B. Complete—Acts 8:17. All Christians are indwelt with the Holy Spirit, but none have the fulness until they speak in tongues. No one in the early church received the baptism of the Holy Spirit without speaking in tongues.

C. Consistent—Acts 15:7-8. This experience was consistent with all Christians in the early church.

IV. THE POWER OF THE BAPTISM

A. Witnessing power—Acts 1:8, Acts 4:31. This power changed Peter from a reed to a rock. He denied Christ, but in a short time he was filled with the Spirit and was a powerhouse (Acts 2:41).

B. Working power—I Corinthians 12:4-11, 28. These gifts are given to Spirit-filled Christians to carry on God's work.

C. Worshiping power—Galatians 5:22-23. These fruits of the Spirit help Christians live Spirit-filled lives.

D. Warning power—Mark 16:20. The Spirit gave the early church power to warn others against sin and Satan.

Have you received the Holy Spirit? (Note the question of Acts 19:2.) This question was asked to people who had already been born again. The baptism of the Holy Spirit is something more than salvation. The power of Spirit baptism aids Christians in daily living and in their work for God.

8.

THE EVIDENCE OF THE
BAPTISM OF THE HOLY SPIRIT
Mark 16:17

Many try to disprove the fact that speaking in tongues is for today by taking Scriptures out of context to prove their points. Despite this opposition, many have received the baptism of the Holy Spirit with the evidence of speaking in tongues. God fills all who are hungry and seeking this experience, providing they obey His Word.

I. **THE PROMISE OF THE BAPTISM**
  A. Pouring out the Spirit—Joel 2:28-29. Though this Scripture does not say, "speaking in tongues," it is implied.
  B. Proof of the Holy Spirit—Acts 2:4; 10:45. All 120 people in the upper room, including women, spoke in tongues. No one received the baptism of the Holy Spirit without speaking in tongues.
  C. Prophet's promise—Isaiah 28:11. This promise was made 700 years before Christ was born.

II. **THE PURPOSE OF THE BAPTISM**

A. Proof of the baptism of the Holy Spirit—John 15:26; Acts 2:4. Again, no one received the baptism of the Holy Spirit without speaking in tongues.

B. Planned by God for the Church—I Corinthians 12:28; 14:21. This was God's plan for the church then and still is His plan today.

C. Proof of the resurrection and glorification of Christ—John 16:7; Acts 2:22, 32-33. Christ promised He would send the Comforter. When the Spirit descended, it was proof that Christ was glorified.

D. Private worship by talking to God—I Corinthians 14:2. This is not the same as tongues that should be interpreted.

E. Praying by speaking in tongues—Romans 8:26; I Corinthians 14:2, 14. Many times the Spirit intercedes for others by praying through us in another language.

III. THE POWER OF THE BAPTISM

A. Sign to the believer—John 7:38-39; Mark 16:17. Jesus said all believers could speak in tongues (Mark 16:17).

B. Sign to the unbeliever—I Corinthians 14:22. Many non-Christians are convicted by this experience and receive Christ.

C. Spiritual edification—I Corinthians 14:4. This means to "be built up" spiritually into a stronger Christian.

D. Spiritual edification for the church—I Corinthians 14:5.

IV. THE PROBLEMS OF THIS BAPTISM

A. Rejection. The Bible says that speaking in tongues is for today and is to be practiced (I Cor. 14:39).

B. Reasoning away. Although some use reasoning to try to prove that speaking in tongues is not for today, the Bible says it is for all people, everywhere (Acts 2:39; I Cor. 14:5).

9.

THE HOLY SPIRIT IN THE BELIEVER
John 16:7

I. **THE HOLY SPIRIT IN CONVICTION**—John 16:8-11
   A. He convicts people of sin—vv · 8, 9. Men are born in sin—Romans 3:23. The Holy Spirit shows man he is a sinner and that he should turn to God's goodness.
   B. He convicts the world of sin—v. 9. The sin of the world is unbelief and rejection of Christ.
   C. He offers deliverance from judgment—v. 10. Because Christ ascended into heaven and the Comforter came, righteousness is available for those who turn to God.
   D. He convicts the person of sin—v. 11. Satan has already been judged.

II. **THE HOLY SPIRIT IN CONVERSION**
   A. Pardon by Spirit—John 3. Being born of the water and the Spirit, is the only way to enter God's kingdom. The water stands for refreshment and the Spirit provides redemption and regeneration.
   B. Power of the Spirit—Titus 3:5. We had nothing to do with our salvation, other than accepting Christ. It is the Spirit that regenerates and makes man a new creature in Christ. Paul speaks of this in II Corinthians 5:17.
   C. Practice of the Spirit—Ezekiel 36:26. God places within man a new spirit.

III. **THE HOLY SPIRIT IN CLEANSING**
   A. Saved by the Savior—II Corinthians 5:17. Notice the importance of "being in Christ."
   B. Secured by the Spirit—Romans 8:16. The Spirit gives evidence that we are the children of God.

IV. THE HOLY SPIRIT IN CONTROLLING

The Holy Spirit wants to control God's people, however He will not force Himself upon any man.

A. Favor of the Spirit—I John 4:13. We are assured that we are children of God by having His Spirit dwelling in us.

B. Fruit of the Spirit—Galatians 5:22, 23. The nine fruits come as the result of being filled with and living in the Spirit.

V. THE HOLY SPIRIT IN COMPLETION

A. Healing for the soul. Jesus spoke of man losing his soul (Mark 8:36). However, through faith, we can have our souls restored. David spoke of this in Psalm 23:3.

B. Healing for the body—Isaiah 53:5. Christ paid the price for our healing. He wants us to be healthy.

C. Healing for the mind. We keep our minds healthy by allowing the Holy Spirit to control them. (See Psalm 19:14.)

10.

THE PERSONALITY
OF THE HOLY SPIRIT
John 16:7-14

I. THE HOLY SPIRIT SAVES—John 3:5

A. He convicts man of his need of a Savior.

B. He convinces man of his need of a Savior.

C. He converts (changes) man. As man is in Christ, he is a new person (II Cor. 5:17). This is brought about by the Spirit.

II. THE HOLY SPIRIT SANCTIFIES—Romans 15:16

We do the confessing; He does the cleansing.

A. He sanctifies through the Scriptures (Ps. 119:9, 11).

B. He sanctifies through surrender. As we surrender to Christ, His blood keeps cleansing us (I John 1:7).

C. He sanctifies through separation. As we cooperate with the Holy Spirit, we will live a clean life (II Cor. 7:1).

III. THE HOLY SPIRIT SEARCHES—I Corinthians 2:10

A. He searches man's actions. He knows how we act.

B. He searches man's ambitions. He knows our desires and plans.

C. He searches man's affections. He knows of our love.

D. He searches man's attitudes. He knows our thoughts and feelings.

Allow Him to search you and cleanse you daily.

IV. THE HOLY SPIRIT STRENGTHENS—Acts 1:8

A. Strength to follow. The Christian life may be hard to live, but the Spirit gives us strength as we pray.

B. Strength to fight. The Christian life is a battleground. With the help of the Spirit, and God-given tools we can be a success in the Christian life (Eph. 6:10-18).

C. Strength to fellowship. The Holy Spirit gives us strength to attend the house of God. It is important to attend church, because the Holy Spirit is there to quicken and strengthen us (Heb. 10:25).

V. THE HOLY SPIRIT SEALS—Ephesians 1:13

A. The Spirit owns our time. Give Him all your time.

B. The Spirit owns our talent. Use them for His honor.

C. The Spirit owns our tithes. Give your money to Him.

VI. THE HOLY SPIRIT SOOTHES—John 16:7

A. Comfort in sorrow. The Holy Spirit gives strength to accept God's will.

B. Comfort in sickness. If you are not healed, be patient.

C. Comfort in separation. When losing a loved one, He comforts us.

VII. THE HOLY SPIRIT SIMPLIFIES—John 16:13

A. He reveals the Scriptures to us and helps us understand them.

B. He reveals the Savior. He makes Jesus real to us.

God is looking for people who will be instruments in the hands of the Holy Spirit. As people yield to the Spirit, He takes them and works in them, making them effective workers for the Lord. God is not looking for intelligence or talent as much as He is looking for consecration. Learn to yield to Him.

11.

THE WORK OF THE HOLY SPIRIT
Acts 1:8; Acts 2:1-4

The Holy Spirit wants to work in the hearts and lives of men and women. He can do more for us in a few moments than we can do for ourselves in our lifetime. He wants to fill us, empower us, guide us, and work through us.

I. PURGING POWER—John 16:8

A. He purges from sin. This is salvation.

B. He purges from unrighteousness. This is holiness.

C. He purges from judgment. This is assurance.

II. PRAYING POWER—Romans 8:26

A. He helps us in our weakness. He gives spiritual strength.

B. He prays through us. This is intercession.

III. **PARDONING POWER**—Romans 8:16
   A. He convicts—Acts 2:37. God planned our salvation. Jesus paid for our salvation. The Holy Spirit brings our salvation.
   B. He cleanses—Acts 2:38. Note Peter's words: "for the remission of sins."

IV. **PREACHING POWER**
   A. Power to witness—Acts 1:8. This power was promised to the disciples to help them do God's work. The disciples were helpless without this power.
   B. Power to work—Acts 4:31. They were given power to speak the Word of God.

V. **PRAISING POWER**—John 16:14
   A. Praise through prayer—Acts 3:1-12
   B. Praise through preaching—Acts 2:14-41. Peter's preaching lifted up Christ.
   C. Praise through worship as a form of praise—Acts 2:46-47.

VI. **PERCEIVING POWER**—John 16:15
   1. The Spirit helps us understand God's will for our lives.
   2. The Spirit shows us the meaning of God's Word.
   3. We can understand God's personality and power by the help of the Spirit.

VII. **PERSONAL POWER**—John 14:26
   A. Power to teach us. He shows us right from wrong.
   B. Power to train us. He helps us remember.

VIII. **PACIFYING POWER**—John 15:7
   A. Comfort in sorrow—Ephesians 6:22
   B. Comfort during separation—Matthew 28:20
   C. Comfort when sick—Psalm 30:1-3. If God does not choose to heal a sick person, He will give that person power to endure.

12.

SINS AGAINST THE HOLY SPIRIT
Genesis 6:3

Men can and do sin against the Holy Spirit. Indifferent attitudes or rebellious spirits often lead men to sin against the Spirit. Sometimes as the result of misunderstanding, men sin against the Spirit.

I. **REJECTING THE SPIRIT**—Isaiah 63:10
   A. Rejecting His plan—Genesis 6–8. The animals obeyed God and went into the ark, but men refused to obey.
   B. Rejecting His pleadings—Proverbs 29:1. If men reject God's pleas, they will be suddenly cut off.
   C. Rejecting His pardon—II Corinthians 6:2. Today is the day for men to be sure of salvation and pardon.

II. **BLASPHEMY AGAINST THE SPIRIT**—Matthew 12:31-32
   A. Sin against the Savior—v. 31. If a person sins against the Savior, he will be forgiven.
   B. Sin against the Spirit—v. 32. If a person sins against the Holy Spirit he will not be forgiven.

Although a person may not agree with certain teachings of the Holy Spirit, that person should never oppose the Spirit, since he may be guilty of blasphemy.

III. **LYING AGAINST THE SPIRIT**—Acts 5:1-10
   A. Design—vv. 1-2. Ananias and Sapphira lied, saying they gave all the money they received from selling their home to the church.
   B. Destruction—vv. 3-5. Ananias, the husband, dropped dead after he lied to Peter and the Holy Spirit.
   C. Degradation—vv. 6-10. Sapphira, the wife, not knowing her husband died from lying, also lied and was struck dead.

IV. **GRIEVING THE HOLY SPIRIT**—Ephesians 4:30
There are many ways which man grieves the Spirit.
Here are some:
   A. Unchristian conduct—Galatians 5:16. If we
   walk in the Spirit, we will not obey the lusts of
   the world. When filled with the Spirit, we
   should practice walking in the Spirit.
   B. Unholy conduct—Galatians 5:17. The flesh
   opposes the Spirit. Self always leads to unholy
   attitudes and unholy conduct.
   C. Unchristian control—Galatians 5:19-21. Here
   we see the works of the flesh. Note the difference between the works of the flesh than
   the fruits of the Spirit (Gal. 5:22-23).

V. **QUENCHING THE SPIRIT**—I Thessalonians 5:19
   A. Do not quench His promptings. The Spirit
   prompts men to pray, witness, and step out in
   faith.
   B. Quenching His progress—Acts 2:13. Some
   thought these people were drunk. Many refuse
   the work of the Spirit.
   C. Quenching His power—John 9:1-25. Many
   question the healing of the blind man. Though
   healed, many doubt and question God's power.

13.

PERSONAL PENTECOSTAL POWER
Acts 1:8

Before Christ ascended into heaven, He promised to send
the Comforter (John 16:7). While on earth Christ could
be at only one place at a time. However, after He
ascended into heaven and the Holy Spirit descended,
the Spirit could be with all men at all places at all
times. Note the promised power (Acts 1:8). This power
changed the disciples. It took failures and made them
great successes.

I. **POWER TO SING**—Acts 16:22-33
   A. Punishment—vv. 22-24. Paul and Silas were put in prison and placed in stocks as punishment for preaching the gospel.
   B. Praise—v. 25. At midnight they sang praises to God.
   C. Power—vv. 26-29. An earthquake shook the prison, causing the jailor to become fearful, for he thought the prisoners had escaped.
   D. Pardon—vv. 30-33. The jailor was convicted of his sin. He asked, "What must I do to be saved?" Paul gave him the answer. That night the jailor and his family was converted and baptized.

II. **POWER TO SURRENDER**—Acts 15:26
   A. Surrender—Acts 5:29. Better to obey God than man.
   B. Suffering—II Corinthians 11:24-27. Note Paul's surrender. He was one of the most dedicated men of all times.
   C. Sacrifice—Acts 5:41. These followers of Christ counted it an honor to suffer and sacrifice for the Lord.

III. **POWER TO SPEAK**—Acts 3:1-16
   A. Prayer for power—v. 1. Peter and John went to the temple to pray.
   B. Person in need of power—v. 2. A man who was crippled from birth begged them for money.
   C. Power given to the person—vv. 3-7. The cripple was healed.
   D. Power brings praising—vv. 8-9. He rejoiced in his healing.
   E. People wonder at the power—vv. 10-11. Bystanders didn't understand.
   F. Preaching explains the power—vv. 12-16. Peter explained the reason for the miracle.

IV. **POWER TO SAVE**
   A. Peter's shame—Luke 22:57-60. Peter denied

Christ three times. Peter could boast, but not stand for the Lord.

B. Peter's sincerity—Acts 1:1-26. Peter was later one of the 120 in the upper room who experienced the power of the Holy Spirit (Acts 2:1-4).

C. Peter's sermon—Acts 2:37-41. Peter became a new man. He preached and 3,000 were saved.

V. POWER TO SERVE

A. Seeing the lost—Acts 17:16. Paul saw the sinful city and was stirred within his spirit.

B. Searching the lost—Acts 20:20. They went from house to house with the gospel, changing their world.

C. Sorrow over the lost—Acts 20:31. They shed tears over the lost.

D. Saving the lost—Acts 2:47. Souls were added to the church daily. Winning souls was Paul's first desire and ambition.

The Holy Spirit changes weakness to power, indifference to faithfulness, shyness to boldness, and failures to success. Paul warned, "Be filled with the Spirit" (Eph. 5:18).

14.

THE POWER OF PENTECOST
Acts 17:6

Pentecost not only changed the church world, but the secular world as well. Within thirty-two years after Pentecost, most of the then-known world had heard about Christ. The people of that time had no printing presses, church literature, church buildings, or automobiles to help spread the gospel. Nevertheless, the Spirit filled the believers and gave them ambition and determination to do God's work. We can have the same power today.

I. **CHANGING POWER**
   A. Personalities changed—II Corinthians 5:17. When a person is saved, he experiences a change in attitude, actions, and ambition. His heart and personality are changed (Ezek. 36:26).
   B. Purpose changed. The purpose of the believers' lives changed from selfishness to service. They went from house to house, serving others (Acts 5:42). They didn't have a desire to be served; they wanted to serve.
   C. Practices changed—Acts 8:1-3; 9:1-16. Saul the persecutor changed into a preacher. Note that after his conversion "straightway he preached Christ in the synagogues, that he is the Son of God" (Acts 9:20).

II. **COMPASSIONATE POWER**
   See Paul's compassion in Acts 20:31. Compassion is more than love; it is love in action.
   A. Compassion grows—Acts 20:31. Paul shed tears for three years.
   B. Compassion groans—Romans 8:26. The Spirit prays in us.
   C. Compassion gives—Acts 21:13. Paul was ready to give his life for the cause of Christ.
   D. Compassion goes—Mark 16:15. Obeying Christ's command to tell others the good news.

III. **CONVERTING POWER**
   To convert means "to change."
   A. Conversion from a life of sin—Acts 2:41. Some of those who helped crucify Christ were among the 3,000 converted.
   B. Conversion from the power of Satan—Acts 19:19. Evil books were destroyed. God is much more powerful than Satan (I John 4:4).
   C. Conversion from a life of slavery—Acts 15:1-20. Men were no longer under the law, but under grace.

IV. CONTINUING POWER

"They joined with the other believers in regular attendance at the apostles' teaching sessions and at the Communion services and prayer meetings" (Acts 2:42, LB).

What did the apostles teach?

A. Salvation—Acts 4:12; 16:31. Christ is the one true way of salvation.

B. Surrender—Acts 26:19. Paul was not disobedient to the heavenly vision.

C. Suffering—Acts 5:41. The believers were happy to suffer for the sake of the gospel.

D. Sacrifice—Acts 15:26. Judas and Silas endangered their lives for the sake of the gospel.

15.

A SPIRIT-FILLED SERMON
Acts 2:14-16, 22-24, 31-41

I. ELEMENTS OF A GOOD SERMON

A. Prayer. Prayer by the pastor as he studies, as well as support from the congregation is needed to make a power-packed sermon.

B. Scripture. When the Scriptures are used in a sermon, there will be results (Heb. 4:12).

C. Reception. The listeners must be interested in hearing the Word. Regardless of the speaker or sermon content, the sermon will not be a success unless the people are receptive.

II. THE INTRODUCTION—vv. 14-16

A. Person—v. 14. Peter, who had denied the Lord seven weeks earlier, was now a new man. What made the difference? He was one of the 120 people in the upper room who received the Holy Spirit.

B. Problem—v. 15. The Christians were not drunken as the non-Christians suspected.

C. Prophecy—v. 16. The prophecy of Joel 2 28, 29 was now being fulfilled. The people in the New Testament would experience the fulness of the Holy Spirit.

III. THE IMPACT—vv. 22-24
A. Proof—v. 22. Christ was approved of God. Christ was not only the Son of God, but the promised Messiah. He proved this by His miracles and wonders. Peter used Psalm 16:8-11 in his sermon.
B. Prophecy—v. 23. Christ was crucified according to the Old Testament Scriptures (Isa. 53; Ps. 22). Though these men were sinful, they fulfilled the Old Testament Scriptures.
C. Power—v. 24. Christ overcomes death. He came to give life (John 10:10). He is victorious over death.

IV. THE INSPIRATION—vv. 31-36
A. Remembrance—v. 31. God did not forget Christ (Acts 2:24-30). If Christ had not risen, His words and teachings would have been proven untrue.
B. Resurrection—vv. 32-33. After the resurrection, Christ was on earth for forty days. He then ascended into heaven (Acts 1:9-12). He is now sitting at the right hand of God.
C. Reality—vv. 34-36. David is not speaking of himself; He is speaking of Christ. (Note v. 36, that the Jews had crucified Jesus who was the Lord and Christ.)

V. THE INVITATION—vv. 37-39
A. People—v. 37. The people were convicted. They asked what they needed to do to be saved.
B. Plan—v. 38.
  1. Repent. Change your way of living.
  2. Be baptized as an outward sign of your salvation.

3. You will receive the baptism of the Holy
　　　　Spirit.
　C. Promise—v. 39. This promise (salvation and
　　　the gift of the Holy Spirit) is to all people of all
　　　generations.

16.

REACHING THE LOST
THROUGH PENTECOST
Acts 2:24-47

I.　**PENTECOSTAL PRAYING**

　A. Purpose of praying—Luke 24:49. Command to
　　　wait and seek the Lord's will.
　B. Promise of praying—Acts 1:8. Power from the
　　　Holy Spirit came through prayer.
　C. Privacy of prayer—Matthew 6:6. Secret pray-
　　　ing brings rewards from God.
　D. Power of prayer—Acts 3:1-8. God gives men
　　　supernatural power to help others because of
　　　prayer.
　E. People who prayed:
　　　1. Elijah—I Kings 18 (cf. James 5:17).
　　　2. Jacob—Genesis 32:24-28. Jacob's name as
　　　　well as character changed.
　　　3. Moses—Exodus 24:18. Moses prayed for
　　　　forty days.
　　　4. Daniel—Daniel 6:10. Daniel prayed three
　　　　times daily.
　　　5. Church—Acts 12:1-15. Peter was freed
　　　　from prison because of the prayers of his
　　　　friends.

Prayer is not only speaking, but is listening and
waiting before God (Isa. 40:31).

II.　**PENTECOSTAL PREACHING**

　A. Plain preaching—II Corinthians 3:12. Simpli-
　　　city is needed more than ever. Such preaching

meets all the needs of man.
  B. Powerful preaching. The anointing of the Holy Spirit
    a) Paul—I Corinthians 2:4. Paul preached in demonstration and power of the Spirit.
    b) Paul—Ephesians 5:18. To be effective preachers need to be filled with the Spirit.
    c) Zechariah—Zech. 4:6. God's work is not accomplished by force, but by the power of the Holy Spirit.
    d) David—Psalm 92:10. David desired to be anointed with fresh oil.
    e) John—I John 2:20. God anoints men to do His work.
    f) Jesus—Luke 4:18. Jesus was anointed to preach the gospel.
    g) Peter—Acts 10:44. The Holy Spirit fell as Peter spoke.
    h) Peter and John—Acts 4:13. Men saw Christ in Peter's and John's lives.
  C. Preaching that purges—John 16:8. Preaching exposes sin in the lives of Christians and sinners.

III. PENTECOSTAL POWER
  A. Convicting power—Acts 16:30-31. No sermon was preached, yet the jailor was convicted and converted.
  B. Consecrating power—Acts 15:26. The people risked their lives for the sake of the gospel.
  C. Curing power—Acts 3:1-8; 5:15; 19:11-12. Healing is available for all today.

IV. PENTECOSTAL PASSION
  A. Concerned passion—Acts 5:42. The apostles went everywhere preaching the gospel.
  B. Constrained passion—I Corinthians 9:16. Paul was so moved that he could do nothing but preach the gospel.
  C. Crying compassion—Acts 20:31. Paul shed tears for the lost for three years.

V. THREE-FOLD VISION

    A. Of God. We need to always remember that God is holy.

    B. Of self. We are nothing without God's help.

    C. Of the lost. We need to see the needs of the lost. Three things hinder us from meeting their needs.

        1. Indifference

        2. Lack of vision

        3. Lack of power

17.

THE HOLY SPIRIT AND THE CHURCH

It is the desire of God that the Holy Spirit be the leader of the church. It was the Holy Spirit who established the church on the day of Pentecost. It was the Spirit who maintained the church in the book of Acts, as well as throughout history. When the Spirit has His rightful place within the church, the church will be a powerhouse for God, changing the world as the early church did.

I. PREPARING THE CHURCH—I Corinthians 12:13

    A. The Spirit. "For by one spirit are we all baptized into one body" (v. 13a). Jesus told Nicodemus that men must be born of the Spirit and of water in order to enter God's kingdom (John 3:5). When we are born into God's family, He is our Father and we are His children (John 1:12).

    B. The scope. ". . . whether we be Jews or Gentiles, whether we be bond or free" (v. 13b). Salvation is for whosoever shall call on the name of the Lord (John 3:16; Rom. 10:13). The Spirit calls all men to salvation. Those who respond and accept Christ, become members of

God's family, as well as His church.

C. The sharing. "And have been all made to drink into one Spirit" (v. 13c). Church customs and rituals mean little to God. All who have been born again are members of His family.

II. PERSONALITY OF THE CHURCH—Ephesians 2:20-22

A. Foundation of the church—v. 20. The church is built upon the apostles and the prophets with Christ as the chief cornerstone, not upon a man, an organization, nor a dogma. Matthew 16:18 tells how Christ would build His church upon the rock.

B. Frame of the church—v. 21. The church must be properly put together and must be holy in the sight of the Lord. Paul spoke of the holiness of the church in Ephesians 5:25-27.

C. Fellowship of the church—v. 22. Note the four-fold fellowship:
1. Fellowship with God—I John 1:7a
2. Fellowship with Christ—I John 1:7c
3. Fellowship with the Spirit—through prayer and praise
4. Fellowship with Christians—I John 1:7b

III. POWER OF THE CHURCH

A. Praying power—Luke 24:49. Note the importance of these words: pray, wait, tarry. The power of prayer is shown in Acts 4:31.

B. Preaching power—Acts 1:8. See Peter in Acts 2 preaching with authority. Just a short time before he had denied Christ, now he is changed. The Holy Spirit made the difference.

IV. PROVISION FOR THE CHURCH

The Holy Spirit provides proper leadership for the church.

A. The selection of leaders—Acts 13:2-4. The Holy Spirit knows who is best qualified for certain jobs and selects accordingly.

B. The sacredness of leadership—Acts 20:28. The Holy Spirit appoints certain men to take care of the flock of God.
C. The stability of leaders—II Corinthians 6:4-6. Sufferings, misunderstandings, and even pain are part of being a leader.

It has been said that the success of the early church was three-fold: Jesus went up; the Holy Spirit came down; and the disciples went out.

18.

THE HOLY SPIRIT, OUR HELPER
John 16:7-14

I. **THE SAVIOR'S WORDS**—v. 7
   A. Departure of the Savior—v. 7a. Christ would ascend to His home in heaven (John 14:1-3). This would be fulfilled in Acts 1:9-11. Christ knew the will of God and the plan for His life.
   B. Descent of the Spirit—v. 7b. If Christ did not go away, the Comforter (the Holy Spirit) would not come.

II. **THE SPIRIT'S WORK**—vv. 8-11
   A. Reproving—v. 8. He would reprove:
      1. Of sin
      2. Of righteousness and unrighteousness
      3. Of judgment
   B. Rebuke—v. 9. Christ would judge sinners, because of their failure to accept His love and pardon. The Bible speaks of the final judgment in Revelation 20:11-15.
   C. Righteousness—v. 10. Christ has gone to the Father. Righteousness is needed in our lives, in our churches, and in our nation.
   D. Revealing—v. 11. The power of Satan will be destroyed.

III. THE SPIRIT'S WAY—vv. 12-14
A. Spiritual ignorance—v. 12. There are things that are too overwhelming for men to know now that are understood by only the Lord and the Holy Spirit.
B. Spirit's impact—v. 13. The Holy Spirit will speak of certain things.
1. Guidance. He will guide men into all truth.
2. Unselfish. He will not speak for Himself.
3. Revelation. He will speak what He hears from God.
4. Prophecy. He will tell future events.
C. Spirit's influence—v. 14
1. The Spirit will praise Christ. "He shall glorify Me."
2. The Spirit will share Christ. "For He shall receive of mine, and shall show it unto you."

IV. THE SPIRIT CHANGES MEN
A. Attitudes. The Holy Spirit will change once unholy men to Christlike men as He is allowed to work in their lives.
B. Ambitions. The Holy Spirit will give men goals that are pleasing to the Lord.
C. Affections. The Holy Spirit will help men to love Christ and others.
D. Actions. The Holy Spirit will show men how to put their love for Christ and others into action.

19.

THE SPIRIT-FILLED CHRISTIAN
Ephesians 5:18

I. WILL BE *DEVOTED*
A. By study—II Timothy 2:15. We are to hide God's Word in our heart (Ps. 119:11; see also Joshua 1:8; Psalm 119:9).

B. By surrender—Romans 12:1, 2. Our bodies belong to God, therefore our bodies should bring honor and glory unto God. (See I Corinthians 6:19, 20.)

C. By separation—I Timothy 5:22. We are to keep ourselves pure. (Note the words of Paul in II Corinthians 6:17; 7:1.)

II. WILL BE *DEDICATED*

A. Loving God—II Corinthians 11:24-27. Paul's dedication to God caused him to accept all these sufferings. He had scars on his body as the result (Gal. 6:17).

B. Looking to God—Hebrews 12:1, 2. We need to keep our eyes upon Christ. Looking about us will bring discouragement, but looking to Him brings encouragement, strength, and help.

C. Longing for God—Philippians 3:10. Paul had one desire—to know God. Note the desire of Job in Job 23:3. This longing will draw us not only near to God, but make us like Him.

III. WILL BE *DETERMINED*

A. Testimony—Acts 20:24. Paul could say that all sufferings and problems could not move or discourage him.

B. Testings—Galatians 6:9. Suffering for Christ was a test for Paul, yet he endured testing. He was determined to live for the Lord regardless of the cost.

C. Trials—James 5:11. Christians will be happy to endure all the trials that come their way.

D. Temptation—James 1:12. The person who endures temptation is blessed by God, and is a happy person.

IV. WILL BE *DETAINED*

There must be a time of waiting before God in prayer (Isa. 40:31).

A. Plea to prayer—I Timothy 2:8. Men everywhere should pray.

B. Personal prayer—Matthew 6:6. Secret prayer is the secret of the Christian life.

C. Powerful prayer—James 5:16. There is no limit to the power of the prayers of the righteous.

D. Patient prayer—Acts 1, 2. They prayed for ten days. This was Christ's command (Luke 24:49).

E. Prevailing prayer—I Thessalonians 5:17. Christians should always be in the attitude of prayer.

20.

THE SPIRIT-FILLED CHURCH
Acts 2:41-47

What is a Spirit-filled church? The best way to measure is to look at the early church of the book of Acts.

I. A *GROWING* CHURCH
"And the Lord added to the church daily such as should be saved" (Acts 2:47b).

A. Growth in attention—Acts 2:42. They continued in the apostles' doctrine which was true to God's Word.

B. Growth in attendance—Acts 2:46. They were daily in the temple.

C. Growth in affection—Acts 2:45. They sold their possessions and shared their money

D. Growth in attitude—Acts 5:29. They would rather obey God and suffer than obey men.

II. A *GOING* CHURCH
"And daily in the temple, and in every house, they ceased not to teach and preach Jesus Christ" (Acts 5:42).

A. People could not stop them—Romans 1:16. Paul was not ashamed of the gospel; criticism could not stop him.

B. Prisons could not stop them—Philippians 4:11. Wherever he was, Paul was content. Paul

and Silas were even happy in prison (Acts 16:20-33).
C. Persecution could not stop them—Acts 20:24. Paul could say that despite his sufferings, nothing would make him give up Christ.
D. Problems could not stop them—Acts 6:1-15. All threats, and even murder, could not stop Stephen from serving Christ.

III. A *GLOWING* CHURCH

The early believers changed their world (Acts 17:6).
A. The power—Acts 11:26. It was the world that called Christ's followers Christians.
B. The prayer—Acts 4:13. Peter and John, though ignorant, showed Christ within them. This came as the result of prayer.
C. The persuasion—Acts 26:28. This power of the Spirit caused people to do some serious thinking. The apostles had the power of Acts 1:8.

IV. A *GROANING* CHURCH

A. Crying for the lost—Acts 20:31. Paul's love for the non-Christian caused him to weep for the lost.
B. Concern for the lost—Romans 8:26. The Spirit intercedes for those who pray for the lost.
C. Compassion for the lost—II Corinthians 5:11. Knowing the judgment of God (Rev. 20:11-15), we seek to lead men to a saving knowledge of Christ. The psalmist tells us in Psalm 126:5, 6 how we should weep for the lost. (See also Isaiah 66:8, Jeremiah 9:1.)

To reach the lost and preach the gospel to every creature (Mark 16:15), the church must be filled with the Spirit. Forms and rituals will not accomplish the Great Commission. Plans, programs, and even finance will not get the job done. As the church is filled with the Spirit, we will reach the lost with the gospel.

21.

THE LARGEST CHURCH IN TOWN
Acts 2:41-47

The first church was the Pentecostal church. God chose to pour His Holy Spirit upon those in the upper room on the day of Pentecost.

I. **THE CITY**—Jerusalem
   A. Shame—Luke 13:34. They saw Jesus performing miracles, yet they did not believe Him. He came to His own people and they rejected Him (John 1:11).
   B. Self-righteousness—Luke 18:10-14. The Pharisees had a form of Christianity based on the old Law. They persecuted Jesus the most. In fact, it was the religious leaders who had Jesus crucified.
   C. Sin—Matthew 27. The people had Barabbas released and asked that Christ be crucified. No one offered to help (Matt. 27:36). Jerusalem was no different than the cities of today. Some who helped crucify Christ were converted on the day of Pentecost.

II. **THE CHRISTIANS**—born-again Christians
   A. Spirit—Acts 2:4. All were filled with the Holy Spirit (cf. Eph. 5:18).
   B. Signs—Acts 2:43. Many wonders were done by the apostles.
   C. Sacrifice—Acts 2:44-45. The believers sold their possessions and gave their money to God's work (cf. Luke 9:23-24).
   D. Suffering—Acts 16:20-31. Although Paul and Silas were in prison, they sang.
   E. Salvation—Acts 2:47. They preached everywhere.
   F. Speaking—Acts 4:31. The Holy Spirit gave them boldness as they spoke because of their prayers.

III. **THE COMMUNICATION**—their message
   A. Repentance—Acts 2:38. Jesus also preached repentance (Luke 13:3)—a change of heart, a change in living, a change in thinking.
   B. Redemption—Acts 2:21. "Whosoever shall call on the name of the Lord shall be saved" (cf. Rom. 10:13).
   C. Redeemer—Acts 4:12. There is only one way to be saved (cf. John 14:6).
   D. Resurrection—Acts 2:27-32. The power of the gospel is in the resurrection of Jesus Christ.

IV. **THE CONVERSION**—power the for Christians
   A. Conversion—Acts 2:41. Souls were added to the church daily.
   B. Conviction—Acts 16:30-31. Note the question, "What must I do to be saved?"
   C. Consecration—Acts 20:24. All persecution and suffering could not make Paul give up serving Christ.
   D. Completeness—Acts 3:1-8. Peter and John healed the crippled man.

The Spirit-filled church will be the largest church in town when people see the power of the Holy Spirit doing great things there.

22.

THE UNITY OF THE SPIRIT
"And when the day of Pentecost was fully come, they were all with one accord in one place" (Acts 2:1).

There is no limit to the power of unity. The book of Acts demonstrates this fact. As the early church used this power, many people were helped and blessed through the miracles that took place. Satan seeks to divide, but the Spirit always unite.

I. **UNITY IN PRAYER**
   A. Prayer with purpose—Acts 1:14. For ten days,

120 people prayed in unity for God's power so that they could help accomplish His work.

B. Promise of prayer—Acts 18:19. There is no limit to the power of united prayer.

C. Power in prayer—Acts 4:31. United prayer brings unusual power (cf. James 5:16).

II. UNITY IN PENTECOST—Acts 2:1

A. United in the purpose of God. They sought God until they had power to do His work (Luke 24:49).

B. United in the desire for the power of God. They knew they could not do God's work in their own strength.

C. United in prayer unto God. They did not depend on any past experience nor on any wisdom or ability of their own. They needed God's power.

III. UNITY IN PERSEVERANCE—Acts 2:46-47

A. Consistent—"And they, continuing daily." Once a week religion was not enough for the early believers; they needed God daily.

B. Concern—"with one accord." Denominational differences did not divide the early believers. They agreed, since they needed God's power to do His work.

C. Conversion—"And the Lord added to the church daily." When men unite to do God's work, God gives them power.

IV. UNITY IN PERSECUTION

A. Pleasure—Acts 5:40-41. The apostles were willing to suffer for the sake of the gospel.

B. Preaching—Acts 8:1. Persecution scattered the Christians, but as they scattered, they preached the gospel. Persecution always strengthens the Christian as well as the church.

C. Power—Acts 4:1-4. The apostles were told not to preach, but they could not remain silent. As the result, many people were converted.

God's work suffers when various denominations cannot agree in working together to advance the kingdom of God. Some people seem to have no concern about the lost world; they only want to further their viewpoints. Time is short. God's people need to unite in reaching and winning the lost to Christ.

23.

A SPIRIT-FILLED LAYMAN
Acts 6:8-10, 7:51-60

Stephen was a layman who was filled with the Spirit. As the result of being filled with the Spirit, he did wonders and miracles. He set an excellent example of meekness for all Christians to follow.

I.   **THE PERSON**—6:8-10
  A. The character—v. 8. Note a three-fold example of Stephen's character:
    1. Full of faith. All Christians should practice faith.
    2. Full of power. He had power over sin, Satan, and self.
    3. Full of miracles. Stephen did great miracles in the power of Holy Spirit.
  B. The confusion—v. 9. These people opposed Stephen. God's people always face opposition by the world.
  C. The consecration—v. 10. Because Stephen was filled with the Spirit, he had wisdom. One of the gifts of the Spirit is the word of wisdom (I Cor. 12:8). Wisdom is:
    1. Knowing what to do. This means being led by the Spirit.
    2. Knowing why we do it. Having a reason for what we do.

3. Knowing when we do it. Knowing what to say at the right time.
4. Knowing how to do it. Not knowing how to do something can hinder God's work.

II.   THE PREACHING—7:51-54

A. People—v. 51. Many Jews were stubborn, resisting the Spirit as their fathers had. Many people know what is right, but they resist because they are stubborn and disobedient.

B. Prophets—v. 52. "Name one prophet your ancestors didn't persecute! They even killed the ones who predicted the coming of the Righteous One—the Messiah whom you betrayed and murdered" (LB). The Jewish people rejected the prophets and Jesus Christ. Now they rejected the message of Stephen.

C. Problem—v. 53. "Yes, and you deliberately destroyed God's laws, though you received them from the hands of angels" (LB). God gave the Ten Commandments to Moses, but the people rejected them.

D. Personality—v. 54. The preaching of Stephen caused anger among the Jewish people.

III.   THE PERFECTION—7:55-60

A. Position—v. 55. Christ, standing at the right hand of God, welcomed Stephen home.

B. Place—v. 56. "And he told them, 'Look, I see the heavens opened and Jesus the Messiah standing beside God, at His right hand!'" (LB).

C. People—vv. 57-58. The people closed their ears and took Stephen outside the city and stoned him to death. Saul, who later became Paul, held the coats of those who stoned Stephen to death.

D. Prayer—v. 59. Stephen prayed, "Receive my spirit."

E. Pardon—v. 60. He asked God to forgive those who were killing him.

24.

FRUIT OF THE SPIRIT #1:
LOVE
"But the fruit of the Spirit is love" (Gal. 5:22).

I. **DIVINE LOVE**—Matthew 22:37
   - A. Love that worships God—John 4:24. This love is shown in our attendance at church, in our Bible reading, in our daily prayer, and in our daily Christian walk.
   - B. Love that waits on God—Isaiah 40:31. The love that causes us to wait on God will in turn cause us to receive strength and power.
   - C. Love that works for God—Mark 16:15. Love will cause us to fulfill the command of Christ. This command will be easy to obey.

II. **DEDICATED LOVE**
   - A. Love for friends—Matthew 22:39. Loving others as we love ourselves is love from God. The natural man cannot have such love.
   - B. Love for foes—Matthew 5:44. We must love those who oppose us and show kindness to those who mistreat us. This may seem difficult, but with God's help we can do it.
   - C. Love for the friendless—John 13:35. We show that we love Christ by loving others, not in words, but in deeds.

III. **DOMESTIC LOVE**
   - A. Love that shows—Ephesians 5:25-33. Husbands are to love their wives as Christ loved the church. Women are to love their husbands in the same manner. Love will bring respect and respect will increase love.
   - B. Love that shelters—I Timothy 5:8. If a man does not provide for his family he is worse than an unbeliever. The husband should not only provide materially, but spiritually as well.

IV. **DESCRIPTION OF LOVE**—I Corinthians 13:4-7, 13, LB.
   A. Patient—vv. 4-5. Love is patient and kind. It is never jealous. This patient love comes from God as we obey Him.
   B. Praise—v. 6. Love never rejoices in failures, but in the truth, as well as in the success of others.
   C. Protection—v. 7. Love understands and forgives. It protects from all types of wrong and

   D. Permanent—v. 13. Faith, hope, and love remain. All are important, but love is the greatest. One may have great faith, yet not have love, or one may have hope, yet not have love.

25.

FRUIT OF THE SPIRIT #2:
JOY
"But the fruit of the Spirit is joy" (Gal. 5:22).

I. **THE PLAN OF JOY**
   A. Christ's birth brought joy—Luke 2:10. Christ brought good tidings of great joy to all people.
   B. Christ's life brought joy—Acts 10:38. Wherever Christ went, He brought joy, through His teaching, ministry, healing, or miracles.
   C. Christ's death brought joy—John 1:36. Because Jesus is the Lamb of God, we no longer need to make sacrifices. Through His death we have full forgiveness.
   D. Christ's resurrection brought joy—John 14:19. Because He lives, we too shall live (cf. John 11:25, 26).
   E. Christ's ascension brought joy. Note Christ's words before His ascension (John 14:1-3) and the angel's words after Christ's ascension (Acts 1:11).

II. **THE POWER OF THIS JOY**

He wants our joy to be full (John 16:24).

A. Joy in sorrow. Job's life.
   1. Job lost all that he had (Job 1:21).
   2. Job had faith in God (Job 12:15).
   3. He knew God was alive (Job 19:25).
   4. When Job was tried, he was as gold in a fire (Job 23:10).
   5. Even in times of sorrow, Christians may find joy in the Lord (Ps. 30:5).

B. Joy in sickness. (Paul had a thorn in the flesh (II Cor. 12:9). Paul knew that God had a plan and purpose in everyday happenings of men (Rom. 8:28).

C. Joy in suffering—II Timothy 3:12. Persecution and suffering will come. Paul and Silas were in prison, yet they still sang praises to God (Acts 16:25).

III. THE PERIL OF THIS JOY

One may lose the joy of the Lord. David prayed for God to restore the joy of salvation (Ps. 51:12). One may lose this joy:

A. Anger. When one becomes angry, he loses the joy of the Lord.

B. Criticism. Being critical toward others shows the lack of the joy of the Lord.

C. Sin. Sin always separates men from God, causing them to lose the joy of the Lord. David is an example.

D. Spiritual pride. This leads to criticism, as well as a fighting spirit.

E. Lack of patience. A patient person is a joyful person.

26.

FRUIT OF THE SPIRIT #3:
PEACE
"But the fruit of the Spirit is peace" (Gal. 5:22).

I. **SALVATION**
   - A. Peace because of our faith—Isaiah 26:6. By living close to God, we can have peace in our heart, life, and home.
   - B. Peace because of forgiveness—John 5:24. Since all our sins are forgiven, we do not have to be afraid to stand before God.
   - C. Peace because of following. He calls us to follow Him (Matt. 4:19). He then makes us what He wants us to be.
   - D. Peace because of fellowship—I John 1:7. Knowing that we are cleansed from all sin, we can enjoy fellowship with other Christians.

II. **SECURITY**
   - A. Our minds are free from worry—Philippians 4:7. He gives us peace in our hearts, souls, and minds.
   - B. Our minds are free from doubt if we trust God —Hebrews 11:1. We may not understand, but we trust Him in all things.
   - C. Our minds are free from unbelief. We please God by our faith (Heb. 11:6).
   - D. Our minds are free from fear—Isaiah 41:1. Fear destroys faith and trust in God.

III. **SATISFACTION**
   - A. Peace—Psalm 29:11. The Lord will give peace to those who dedicate their lives to Him.
   - B. Promise—Isaiah 26:3. His strength and power keep us.
   - C. Power—John 16:33. In the world there will be trials and tribulation. However, Christ has overcome the problems of the world. He will give us peace.

D. Partition—Ephesians 2:14. He is our peace. Though we were once separated from God, Christ made a way for us to come back to God.

IV. SERENITY
A. Rest—Colossians 3:15. When God rules our hearts, we will have peace.
B. Redemption—Colossians 1:20. Through His blood we have not only forgiveness, but peace.
C. Relaxation—Romans 5:1. Because we are justified we have peace and a relaxed attitude at all times.

27.

FRUIT OF THE SPIRIT #4:
PATIENCE
"But the fruit of the Spirit is longsuffering [patience]"
(Gal. 5:22).

I. PATIENT IN TEMPTATION
A. Reason for temptation—I Corinthians 10:13. Be patient when you are tempted. God knows how much you can bear and will not allow you to be tempted beyond that. He will give you the strength that is needed to overcome all temptations.
B. Result of temptation—James 1:2, 3. Temptation teaches patience. Temptation is not sin until one yields to it.
C. Release from temptation—II Peter 2:9. He knows how to deliver the godly from temptation. As we live godly lives, He will free us from all temptation.
D. Rewards in temptation—James 1:12. After we have been tried, He will reward us in heaven, as well as on earth.

II. PATIENT IN TROUBLES
A. Attitude—Romans 12:12. Being patient during

tribulation is one of the hardest things to practice. God doesn't always deliver from trouble, but He will help us go through it. Patience in trouble shows stability.

B. Affect—Hebrews 10:36. All need patience in time of trouble.
1. Patience—"For ye have need of patience."
2. Promise—"After ye have done the will of God, ye might receive the promise."

C. Answer—Psalm 40:1. Note how the psalmist waits patiently on the Lord. He was in no hurry. Isaiah tells the value of waiting before God (Isa. 40:31).

III. PATIENT IN TRIALS

A. The work of patience—James 1:4. We are to allow patience to have her perfect work. Patience not only tests us; it purifies us. It teaches us complete dependence on God and allows God to have His will and way. Trials teach more than a smooth life can.

B. The waiting in patience—James 5:7. Be patient for the coming of the Lord. Though many long for His coming, we must remember He has a timetable. We must be patient, knowing that all our trials will end when He shall appear.

C. The way of patience—Psalm 37:7. God is never late; He is always right on time.

28.

FRUIT OF THE SPIRIT #5:
KINDNESS
"But the fruit of the Spirit is gentleness [kindness]"
(Gal. 5:22).

I. THE PURPOSE OF KINDNESS—Colossians 3:12

A. Kindness is more than words; it is deeds and actions.

B. Humbleness of mind is realizing we are nothing without God.
C. Meekness is putting Christ first.
D. Longsuffering is needed for one to be kind.

II. **THE PRACTICE OF KINDNESS**—Ephesians 4:32
   A. Considerate. "And be ye kind one to another." The Spirit-filled Christian is considerate of both Christians and sinners.
   B. Concern. "Tenderhearted." Kindness leads to charity. Charity is love in action. It sees men's problems, then helps.
   C. Christlike. "Forgiving one another." We need to practice the teaching of Christ by being forgiving.

III. **THE PERSONALITY OF KINDNESS**—I Corinthians 13:4, 5, LB
   A. The patience of kindness—"Love is very patient and kind."
   B. The practice of kindness—"never jealous or envious."
   C. The practicality of kindness—"never boastful or proud."
   D. The pardon of kindness—"It does not hold grudges and will hardly even notice when others do wrong."

IV. **THE PROOF OF KINDNESS**
   A. Joseph—Genesis 50:18-24. Joseph forgave his brothers. He could have sent his brothers to prison for selling him as a slave, but he forgave and forgot the past.
   B. David—II Samuel 18:5. David forgave Absalom who was seeking to kill his father.
   C. Christ—Luke 23:34. Upon the cross, Christ prayed that God would forgive those who were crucifying Him.
   D. Stephen—Acts 7:60. Stephen forgave the religious leaders and others who were stoning him to death.

FRUIT OF THE SPIRIT #6:
GOODNESS
"But the fruit of the Spirit is goodness" (Gal. 5:22).

I. **SUPERNATURAL GOODNESS**
   A. Personality of God—Psalm 25:8. "The Lord is good and glad to teach the proper path to all who go astray" (LB).
   B. Place of goodness—Psalm 33:5. The earth is filled with the goodness of the Lord. Should the Lord remove His goodness, men would be helpless and hopeless.
   C. Pardoning goodness—Romans 2:4. It is God's goodness that leads men to repentance, and salvation. God doesn't have to forgive men of their sin. Men deserve punishment. It is only God's goodness that keeps men from being sent to hell.
   D. Peace and goodness—Psalm 34:8. Here is an invitation to "taste and see" that the Lord is good.

II. **SENSIBLE GOODNESS**
   A. Practical goodness—Luke 6:27. We are to not only love our enemies, but to do good for them. This is not man's nature. Unless man lives in the Spirit, he cannot expect to fulfill God's rules.
   B. Pity and goodness—Romans 12:20. It is easy to be good to those who are good to us and it is easy to help those who will repay us. But when our enemy is hungry we should feed him; if he is thirsty we should give him to drink.
   C. Prayerful goodness—I Thessalonians 5:15. Never return evil for evil. Always return good for evil. Only as we are filled with the Spirit will we be able to practice this.

III. **SPIRITUAL GOODNESS**

"Surely goodness and mercy shall follow me all the days of my life" (Ps. 23:6).

A. Reaping—Galatians 6:6-7. God promises that we will reap what we sow. We are always paid for what we do, whether it be good or evil.

B. Reward—Luke 6:38. If we give, God will give back. This includes our money, time, life, and work. Withhold from God, and He will withhold from you.

C. Results—Ecclesiastes 11:1, 2. "Give generously, for your gifts will return to you later. Divide your gifts among many, for in the days ahead you yourself may need much help" (LB).

30.

FRUIT OF THE SPIRIT #7:
FAITHFULNESS
"But the fruit of the Spirit is faith [faithfulness]"
(Gal. 5:22).

I. FAITHFULNESS IN LIVING FOR CHRIST

A. Disrespect—Luke 6:46. If one truly loves Christ, he will obey and respect Him.

B. Disregard—I John 1:6. We cannot truly say we love God, but not practice our love for Him.

C. Deliverance—John 8:32, 36. Christ sets men free from all sin. After we accept God's gift of salvation, we must do something on our part —we must resist sin and temptation, keeping ourselves pure.

D. Denouncing—Hebrews 12:1, 2. We are to put aside all things that may hinder us from looking unto Christ, the author and finisher of our faith.

II. FAITHFULNESS IN LOVING CHRIST

A. Complete love—Matthew 22:37, 39. Loving God first, we will love others as we love ourselves.

B. Controlled love—Matthew 6:33. We can have a love strong enough to put Him first in all phases of our lives.

C. Consecrated love—Proverbs 3:5, 6. Here is a very simple, yet safe rule to follow as Christians.

D. Compassionate love—Acts 20:31. A love for Christ will lead to a love for the lost.

III. FAITHFULNESS IN LEARNING OF CHRIST

A. Learning God's will—Psalm 143:10; Romans 12:1, 2. It is easier to find God's will than to do His will.

B. Learning God's Word—Psalm 119:11; Joshua 1:8. Paul tells us to study God's Word (II Tim. 2:15).

C. Learning God's way—Matthew 4:19. As we follow Him, He will make us what He wants us to be.

IV. FAITHFULNESS IN LOOKING FOR CHRIST

A. Promises of His coming—Acts 1:11. He will come the same way He left—in the clouds. We shall rise to meet Him.

B. Person of His coming—John 14:3, "I will come again." There will be no substitute; Christ will come in person.

C. Preparation for His coming—Matthew 24:44. We must be ready at all times for His coming.

31.

FRUIT OF THE SPIRIT #8:
MEEKNESS
"But the fruit of the Spirit is meekness" (Gal. 5:23).

I. PROMISE OF MEEKNESS

A. Practice—Matthew 18:4. Christians should humble themselves like children. Such will be great in heaven.
B. Pleasure—Proverbs 22:4. Note how humility brings a three-fold blessing: riches, honor, and life. Although it is hard to practice meekness, there is great pleasure in practicing it.
C. Paradox—Proverbs 29:23. Pride always brings men down. It makes them low in the sight of their fellowmen, as well as before God. God honors the meek.
D. Personal—Isaiah 57:15. God's Spirit dwells in the life of all who have a meek spirit. Christ brings this meekness; Satan will seek to destroy it.

II. PRACTICE OF MEEKNESS

A. Personal—James 4:10. Humble self. A person does not pray for humility—he practices it. As he humbles himself, God will lift him up.
B. Practice—I Peter 5:5. We are to be clothed with humility.
  1. God resists the proud.
  2. He gives grace to the humble.
C. Practical
  1. Respect—Luke 22:26. Greatness and humility are found in being willing to serve others.
  2. Realization—Romans 12:3. We must not deceive ourselves by thinking we are something we are not.
D. Pleasure—Micah 6:8. Note the requirements from the prophet:
  1. Do justly.
  2. Love mercy.
  3. Walk humbly with God.

III. PEOPLE WITH MEEKNESS

There are many examples, however, here are a few:
A. Joseph—Genesis 50:16-21
B. Saul—I Samuel 9:21

C. David—II Samuel 7:18
D. Solomon—I Kings 3:7
E. John the Baptist—Matthew 3:14
F. Paul—I Timothy 1:15
G. Centurion—Matthew 8:8
H. Syrophenician woman—Matthew 15:27

32.

FRUIT OF THE SPIRIT #9:
SELF-CONTROL
"Meekness, temperance: against such there is no law"
(Gal. 5:23)

I. **CONTROL OF OUR TIME**
   A. Reviewing our time—Psalm 90:12. Knowing the shortness of life, we must adjust our time accordingly.
   B. Remembering the importance of time—Ecclesiastes 12:1. Solomon had all one could ask or dream of, yet he forgot God.
   C. Redeeming the time—Colossians 4:5. "Make most of your chances to tell others the Good News. Be wise in all your contacts with them" (LB).
   D. Realizing the importance of time—Ephesians 5:15-16. "So be careful how you act; these are difficult days. Don't be fools; be wise: make the most of every opportunity you have for doing good" (LB).

II. **CONTROL OF OUR TEMPER**
   A. Patience and anger—Proverbs 16:32. We must control our tempers.
   B. Practical advice—Ecclesiastes 7:9. It is never right to become angry quickly.
   C. Punishment for anger—Matthew 5:22. The punishment for anger is God's judgment.
   D. Practical attention—James 1:19. Christians

should be swift to hear, slow to speak, and slow to anger.

III. CONTROL OF TALENTS—Matthew 25:15-30
A. Reason for talent—v. 15. God expects us to invest our talents or to use them to make a gain.
B. Rules with the talent—vv. 16-18. The five talents increased to ten, the two increased to four, and the one talent was hid in the ground.
C. Rewards for talents—vv. 19-23. God always rewards faithfulness.
D. Rebuke for not using talent—vv. 24-30. If our talents are not used, they will be cast out.

IV. CONTROL OF THE TONGUE
A. Slandering tongue—James 3:5-7. A sharp tongue can destroy others.
B. Surrendered tongue—Ephesians 4:31. All evil is removed from a surrendered tongue.
C. Sanctified tongue—James 1:26. If we do not control our tongues, our religion is vain.

33.

INTRODUCTION TO THE GIFTS
I Corinthians 12:1

God has placed these nine gifts in the church to be used to advance the kingdom of God. They are not to be used for selfish reasons. When God entrusts any of these gifts to a person, that person should not feel spiritually superior.

I. THE PURPOSE OF THE GIFTS
A. To edify. To build up the Christian and the church. Always keep in mind, these gifts are to advance God's work.
B. To encourage. They are to encourage the Christian in every phase of their lives.

C. To enlighten. They help the Christian know right from wrong. Since Satan is supernatural and has power to deceive, we need a supernatural power to understand the true from the false.
D. To educate. These gifts can educate even the illiterate, as they are used for God's glory.
E. To expose. These gifts will help us expose false spirits and religions.

II. THE PERSONALITY OF THESE GIFTS

A. Spiritual gifts vs. natural gifts. Natural gifts are for personal help and enjoyment. Spiritual gifts are to share by helping others.
B. Spiritual gifts vs. fruit of the spirit. Fruit grows; gifts are given.

Spiritual gifts are given by God to those whom He knows will use them for His honor and glory. At times they are given to the most unlikely people. However, only God knows the hearts and minds of men.

III. THE POWER OF THESE GIFTS

A. Power to discern. Spiritual gifts help us discern God's will and way. They also help us discern the nature of a problem, as well as a way to solve that problem.
B. Power to denouce and destroy. Spiritual gifts are backed by the power to denounce the powers of sin, Satan, and sickness.

Some fear the gifts of the Spirit because of past experiences with misuse of the gifts. God has a plan and purpose as to how these gifts are to be given and used. God will give these gifts to those who will use them for His glory.

34.

GIFTS OF REVELATION
I Corinthians 12:8, 10

I. **THE WORD OF KNOWLEDGE**
   A. Explanation. This gift is not human intelligence. It is not knowledge gained from experience, nor is it skill or ability. This gift comes directly from God.
   B. Examples:
      1. John on the island of Patmos is shown future events—Revelation 2–3.
      2. Ananias received revelation of Saul's conversion in complete detail—Acts 9:11-12.
      3. This gift used to expose a hypocrite—II Kings 5:20-27.
      4. The word of knowledge was used to reveal correction for the church—Acts 5:3.
      5. This gift helped the disciples find a suitable meeting place for God's people—Mark 14:13-15.
   C. The word of knowledge may come by means of a dream or vision. However, dreams or visions should always agree with God's Word.

II. **THE WORD OF WISDOM**
   A. Explanation. The word of wisdom is the supernatural revelation by the Spirit for a divine purpose.
   B. Examples:
      1. The wise men needed the word of wisdom to find the Christ child—Matthew 2:20.
      2. God showed His judgment to Noah by a word of wisdom—Genesis 6:13-22.
      3. The word of wisdom was used to assure God's servant of His calling—Exodus 3; Acts 26:16.

III. **DISCERNING SPIRITS**
   A. Explanation. Discerning spirits is a gift given by

the Holy Spirit, enabling a person to instantly discern between the Spirit of God and evil spirits. It is not human intelligence, experience, or ability. It is directly from God. It is not fortunetelling.

B. Evil spirits
1. Satanic spirit—Matthew 24:24. Satan is able to deceive Christians.
2. Seducing spirits—I Timothy 4:1. These spirits are very deceptive. The Bible warns that we should "try the Spirits" (John 4:1).

35.

GIFTS OF POWER
I Corinthians 12:9-10

I. **THE GIFT OF FAITH**
A. Explanation. This is not the faith spoken of in Hebrews 11:6. Paul used the phrase "to another faith" (I Cor. 12:9). It is difficult at times to distinguish between the gift of faith and the gift of the working of miracles.
B. Examples:
1. Personal protection—Daniel 6:16-17, 19-23.
2. Personal provision during a famine—I Kings 17; 19:4-8.
3. Accepting God's promises—Genesis 21:5; Romans 4:20.
4. Deliverances from the lion's den—Hebrews 11:33.
5. Supernatural power—Matthew 17:20.

II. **THE WORKING OF MIRACLES**
A. Explanation. A miracle is a supernatural intervention in the ordinary course of nature. A miracle takes place against natural laws.
B. Examples:
1. The miracles in Egypt—Exodus 7–10.

2. Dividing the Red Sea—Exodus 14:16, 21-22.
3. Miracles of the manna and the water—Exodus 16–17.
4. Elijah and the prophets of Baal—I Kings 18:25-46.
5. Elijah bringing fire from heaven—II Kings 1:9-11.
6. Feeding the 5,000—Matthew 14:15-21.
7. Blinding Elymas—Acts 13:6-11.
8. Transporting Philip—Acts 8:38-39.

III. THE GIFTS OF HEALING

A. Explanation. These gifts are for the supernatural healing of diseases and infirmities without natural means. Instant healing or gradual healing may take place through these gifts.

B. Examples:
1. Laying on of hands—Mark 16:18, 20.
2. Anointing oil and elders—James 5:13-15.
3. Handkerchiefs and aprons—Acts 19:12.
4. Peter's shadow—Acts 5:15.

36.

GIFTS OF INSPIRATION
I Corinthians 12:10

The gifts that confuse people most are the three gifts of revelation. They have at times been misused mainly because of misunderstanding. As the result of this misuse, pastors and laymen have been afraid of use of these gifts. If these gifts are used properly they can be a blessing to individuals, as well as the church as a whole.

I. GIFTS OF PROPHECY

A. Understanding. The Greek word for "prophecy" means to speak for another. Prophecy is a divine inspired and anointed utterance. It is a manisfestation of God without using human knowledge. This gift may be had by all who have received the baptism of the Holy Spirit (I Cor. 14:31).

   B. Use.

      1. For edification, exhortation and comfort— I Corinthians 14:3.

      2. It is not to be used for prediction. God's Word has given us the future.

      3. It is not to be used for personal guidance. Men should use common sense and God's Word for this.

      4. To convict the unbeliever—I Corinthians 14:24-25.

II. GIFT OF TONGUES

   A. Reason for this gift. This gift is to be used for God to speak to men. It is a supernatural utterance never learned by the speaker. These gifts were prophesied by Isaiah and by our Lord (Isa. 28:11-12; Mark 16-17).

   B. Regulations of this gift.

      1. It is used mostly for Christians—I Corinthians 14:23-33.

      2. There is a difference between the baptism of the Holy Spirit (Acts 2:4), and the gift used to help the church. Speaking in tongues in our personal devotion need not be interpreted.

      3. Governing—I Corinthians 14:32, 23-33.

      4. Paul said that we should forbid not to speak in tongues (I Cor. 14:39).

III. GIFT OF INTERPRETATION OF TONGUES

   A. Reason. The gift of interpretation of tongues is used to explain the meaning of the message given in tongues, so that all in the church may be helped (I Cor. 14:5, 27).

   B. Regulation. The one speaking should pray that there be an interpretation (I Cor. 14:13). Only one should interpret the message at one time. No more than three messages may be given in any one service (I Cor. 14:27).